Babysitter Nightmare

Shoo Rayner

Series consultants:
Cliff Moon and Lorraine Petersen

RISING ★ STARS

nasen
NASEN House, 4/5 Amber Business Village, Amber Close,
Amington, Tamworth, Staffordshire B77 4RP

Rising Stars UK Ltd.
22 Grafton Street, London W1S 4EX
www.risingstars-uk.com

The right of Shoo Rayner to be identified as the author of this work has been asserted by him in accordance with the Copyright, Design and Patents Act 1988.

Published 2007

Text, design and layout © Rising Stars UK Ltd.
Cover design: Button plc
Illustrator: Shoo Rayner
Text design and typesetting: Andy Wilson
Publisher: Gill Budgell
Commissioning editor: Catherine Baker
Editor: Clare Robertson
Series consultants: Cliff Moon and Lorraine Petersen

All rights reserved. No part of this publication may be reproduced, stored in a retrieval system, or transmitted in any form by any means, electronic, mechanical, photocopying, recording or otherwise without the prior permission of Rising Stars UK Ltd.

British Library Cataloguing in Publication Data.
A CIP record for this book is available from the British Library

ISBN: 978-1-84680-309-3

Printed by Craft Print International Limited, Singapore

Contents

Characters	4
Scene 1: **The message**	7
Scene 2: **The fear**	19
Scene 3: **The waiting**	29
Scene 4: **The end?**	37
Drama ideas	46

Characters

Amy A teenager who is babysitting for the night.

Lily Amy's best friend. She has some weird ideas.

Danny Lily's boyfriend. He likes to think he's tough.

Characters

Kyle Danny's friend. He's a bit daft sometimes.

Connor Danny's other friend. He loves animals.

Narrator The narrator tells the story.

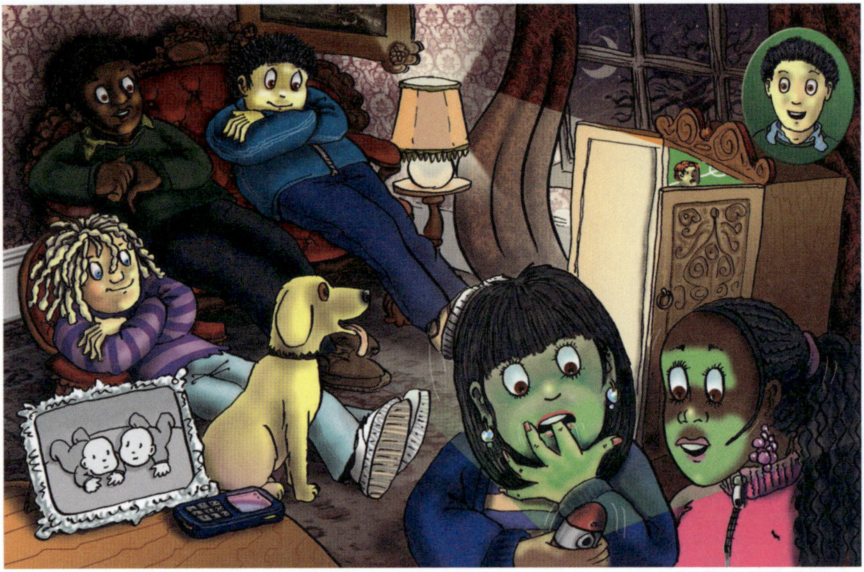

Scene 1

The message

Narrator It is a dark and windy night.
Amy is babysitting at the Petersons'.
Their house is on the edge of town.
It is very big, very old and very posh.

Amy Phew! I thought those babies
would never go to sleep.
Where's my mobile?

Narrator The Petersons' dog, Bonzo,
follows Amy into the sitting room.
Amy writes a text.

Amy "Bbs aslp. Cm n ova."
Send to Lily – done!

Narrator	Amy makes a fuss of Bonzo. He slobbers with joy. The doorbell rings.
Amy	That's quick! Is that you, Lily?
Narrator	There is no reply.
Amy	H-hello! Who's there?
Kyle	Wooooooooh!
Amy	Is that you, Lily? Stop mucking about!
Kyle	Wooooo – woooooo – woooo!
Lily	Kyle, stop being stupid! It's okay, Amy. It's only me. Open up – it's *freezing* out here.

Scene 1   The message

Narrator   Amy opens the door.
Her best friend Lily is there.
Lily's boyfriend Danny and his friends
Kyle and Connor are with her.

Amy   You were quick! Oh no!
Why did you bring those muppets
along? I said to come on your own.
I'm babysitting. It's not a party.

Kyle   Aw, come on Amy – let us in.
I've always wanted to see
what it's like inside this house.

Connor   Yeah. It looks really spooky.
I bet they've got ghosts.

Babysitter Nightmare

Lily Shut up, Connor!

Danny We'll be good, Amy. Promise. Anyway, Lily couldn't come out here all on her own on a night like this.

Lily It *is* spooky out here, Amy. I was a bit scared coming all on my own, you know?

Amy Oh, all right. You'd better take your muddy shoes off.

Narrator Bonzo jumps up and licks Connor's face.

Connor Hello, mate! Who's a good boy, then?

Kyle Ah, isn't that cute? Connor's found a real friend at last!

Scene 1   The message

Narrator   The friends crack up laughing.

Connor   He's gorgeous. What's his name?

Amy   Bonzo.

Connor   Hello, Bonzo!
Can I take him home, Amy?

Amy   No you can't!
And I don't want you guys
taking anything else home
with you, all right?

Danny   Hey, Amy! That's not nice.
We wouldn't do anything like that.
We just want to have a look around.
Wow! This place is like a museum.

Lily	It's like a creepy old movie – *The Addams Family* or something. Everything is so old. I hope they haven't got any skeletons lying around.
Connor	Oh what? They haven't got a telly!
Amy	Yes they have – watch this …
Narrator	Amy opens an antique cupboard. Inside is a plasma TV.
Danny	That is so cool! They've got satellite *and* cable. I wonder what channels they've got. Where's the remote, Amy?
Amy	Please be careful, Danny. Don't break anything.

Scene 1 The message

Danny   It's okay, Amy. I won't break anything.
Hey! They've got all the sports channels!
Look, Connor – it's the City match.
I can't get that channel at home.

Connor   This is my kind of place!
Come on, Bonzo.
Come and sit with me
and watch the match.

Narrator   Amy takes Lily on a tour of the house.
When they get back, the boys
are glued to the TV.

Connor   That was *not* a foul!

Kyle   He's got a yellow card!

Danny   But that striker fell over on purpose.

Kyle   He's acting, Ref!
I don't believe it!
He's been given a penalty!

Lily   Football! That's all you boys
ever think about.

Boys   Uh? What?

Amy   Come through here, Lily.
You've *got* to see the kitchen.

Narrator   The kitchen is full of all
the latest gadgets.

Lily   Wow! This must have cost a fortune.
Mmmmm! Look at the way the drawers
close – so smooth! Oh look,
one of those fold-down TVs – neat!

Amy   I'd love a place like this one day.

Scene 1   The message

Lily   I dunno – all that old stuff
gives me the creeps.
I bet someone died in those
old beds upstairs. I could never sleep
in an old bed.

Amy   You have some strange ideas, Lily.

Lily   Well, old stuff comes from old people.
How do you get the smell out?

Amy   Lily!

Lily   Well … my gran smells old.
They all do at that home of hers.
I hate it. Give me nice, clean,
new stuff any day.

Narrator Amy opens the fridge and looks inside.

Amy Shall we make some pizza?
They said I could help myself.

Narrator As the girls work out how to use the oven, Danny enters. He is waving Amy's mobile.

Danny You've had a text, Amy.

Narrator Amy's face goes pale as she reads the text.

Lily What is it Amy?
What's the matter?

Amy I … er … I …

Lily Let me see.

Scene 1 The message

Narrator Lily grabs the phone and reads the message.

Lily It says, "I'm watching you!"

Danny What? Who sent that?

Narrator Lily scrolls down and reads aloud again.

Lily "*The Teaser*"?
Who's The Teaser, Amy?

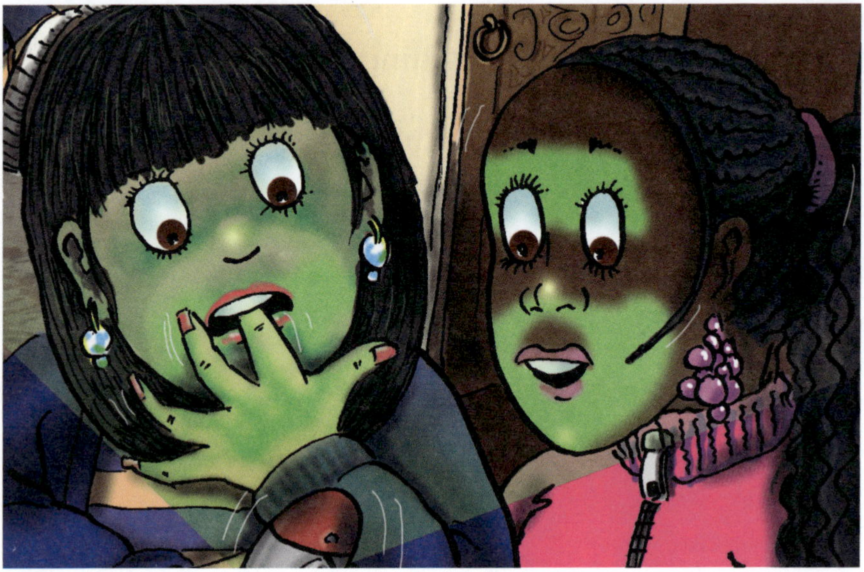

Scene 2
The fear

Narrator	Amy storms into the sitting room.

Amy Right, stop mucking about.
Which one of you sent that text?
It's not funny, you know.

Kyle We wouldn't play a trick
like that, Amy.

Connor Who's The Teaser, Amy?
Mmmm! Amy's got a boyfriend!

Amy That's not funny, Connor.
I bet it's you. Let's see your mobile.
I bet you sent the message.

Danny Right, calm down.
Everyone show Amy the last message
you sent.

Narrator The friends show their last message
folders. None of them sent
the message.

Kyle Well who *did* send it, then?

Connor If The Teaser really is watching you,
maybe he's outside right now.

Narrator Danny goes to the front door
and opens it. The others join him.
As they peer into the darkness,
Amy's phone beeps.

Amy I just don't believe it!
It's him again!

Lily What's it say?

Danny Let me look.

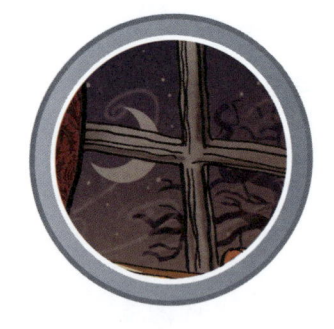

Scene 2 The fear

Narrator Danny reads the text message.

Connor Well?

Kyle Come on … tell us.

Danny It says … "I can see you!"

Amy Eeek! Shut the door and lock it, quick!

Danny Come with me, Connor. Bring Bonzo. We're going to check all the doors and windows. Kyle, you stay here with the girls. Don't move!

Narrator A few minutes later, the oven pings and the pizza is ready. All the friends return to the sitting room to eat.

Danny Well, all the doors and windows are locked. No one can get in.

Kyle   It's got to be someone from school playing a joke. What about Charlene Smith?
She hates you, Amy.

Amy   Nah – she's not clever enough to think up something like this.

Lily   Oh no! Look at that news flash on the bottom of the screen.

Connor   "A dangerous criminal called 'The Teaser' escaped today. Likes to play games with his victims. Beware." *Beware*!

Amy   Did it say "The Teaser"?
We're going to be killed!

Kyle   Calm down, Amy.
I bet it *is* Charlene Smith.
She's really doesn't like you.

Scene 2 The fear

Danny Yeah. She's probably seen the news too.
It's just like her to try and scare you.

Amy Well she's doing a good job.
Anyway, what if it really *is* this Teaser bloke who's sending all these texts?

Lily How could he get hold of your number?
And how does he know
you're babysitting here tonight?
It's not very likely, is it?

Amy Yeah, but – Argh! What's that?

Narrator They hear a scream!
It is Danny's mobile.
A scream is the sound for his text alerts.

Danny Sorry, Amy.
I'll change the alert sound.

Babysitter Nightmare

Babysitter Nightmare

Babysitter Nightmare

Narrator Danny reads his message.
He looks up, terrified.

Danny It can't be. I-i-it's from him –
Th-the Teaser. How's he got hold
of my number too?

Lily It's *got* to be Charlene Smith.
I know she fancies you.
Wait till I see her tomorrow!

Kyle What's it say, Dan?

Danny It says, "Shame about the penalty,
Danny." How does he know
I'm watching the match?

Kyle Oooh! I don't like this.

Connor Me neither! Bonzo's looking
pretty scared too!

Amy I want my dad.

Scene 2   The fear

Narrator   Just then, the room fills with the noise of five mobiles beeping.

All   That's my phone!
I've got a message!

Narrator   They read their messages in silence.
Each message has been sent
by The Teaser.

Danny   This is so weird.
My message just says, "Are".
What do yours say?

Amy   "Sleeping".

Lily   "The".

Kyle   "Babies".

Connor   Mine says, "Hope".
None of it makes sense, does it?

Babysitter Nightmare

Lily Write it down.
Try it in a different order.

Narrator Amy writes down the words
and soon has them sorted.

Amy Hope – The – Babies – Are – Sleeping.
Hope the babies are sleeping!
Oh no! He's after the babies!
Quick – everyone upstairs!

Scene 3
The waiting

Amy Shhh! Quiet!

Narrator Amy and Lily tiptoe up to the cots. The twins are fast asleep.

Lily Ah! Don't they look sweet? They've got no idea what's going on, thank goodness.

Amy I wish I was asleep and this was a dream. I could wake up right now and everything would be all right.

Kyle Yeah, but it's not a dream, is it?
Can you see anything
out of the window, Danny?

Danny No. The wind's blowing the trees
about. There are so many
shadows out there.
It's hard to tell what's what.

Connor Bonzo's scared. Animals can pick up
on these things, you know.
It's like a sixth sense.

Lily Don't say that!

Connor What?

Lily *The Sixth Sense* … Danny made me
watch that movie. It was really creepy!

Connor Oh yeah. That was a great movie.
I really liked the bit where
the little boy –

Scene 3   The waiting

Lily Connor! Shut it!

Danny Yeah, give us a break, Connor.

Connor Oh, right. Sorry Lily.

Kyle What are you doing, Amy?

Amy I'm calling my dad.
He'll come and sort this out.
Come on, pick up the phone …
Oh no, it's the machine.
Yeah, hi Dad. It's me, Amy.
It's nothing, but could you come over when you get this message?

Lily What about the police?
Shouldn't we call them?

Kyle Like they're going to believe there's an escaped nutcase sending us text messages!

Danny But if it *is* him, the police should know.

Amy Wait a minute.
I'll see if I can phone the Petersons …
Come on … come on!
No. No one's answering.
Argh!

Narrator Amy's phone bleeps.
Another text message has arrived.

Amy You read it, Danny.
I can't face it.

Danny I-i-it says, "Don't go back downstairs!"

Scene 3   The waiting

Connor   Right! That's it!
It's time to phone the police.
If you won't do it, I will.

Danny   I'll do it. Nine … Nine … Nine …
hang on … it's ringing.
Hello? Is that the police?

Amy   Here, let me speak to them.

Narrator   Amy takes the phone from Danny.

Amy   Hi? Yeah, I'm babysitting, right?
And I keep getting these messages
from someone calling himself
"The Teaser". He says he's outside
and he's watching us.

Kyle   Tell them we've all had messages.

Amy   There are five of us.
We're getting really scared.
We're upstairs with the babies.
Yeah … Okay … Right … Okay …

Kyle   Ask if they can trace where
he's sending his messages from.

Amy   Can you trace where he's sending
his messages from?

Kyle   Can they do it?

Amy   They're trying right now …
No! Do you think it's really him?
Okay, thanks.

Scene 3   The waiting

Lily What did they say?

Amy The messages were sent
from just outside the house.
We're to stay up here.
They're sending a patrol car over.

Danny Right. Kyle, help me pull this desk
in front of the door.

Connor I'll look out the window
to see when they get here.

Amy No! They said not to do anything
that might tip him off that
they're coming.

Lily You know on the news …
they said he likes to tease his victims?
Well, what do you think he does?
Do you think he's really dangerous?

Danny He's probably just a con man. He scares you out of the house so he can get in and steal stuff.

Kyle *The Teaser* … It doesn't sound very dangerous, does it? Sounds like a comedy villain off Batman.

Lily Cats like to tease their victims before they –

Connor *Bite their heads off and eat them!*

Amy Connor, will you shut up before I –

Narrator The doorbell rings and they hear someone laughing on the doorstep. The noise is terrifying. It sounds like a wild animal caught in a trap.

Scene 4

The end?

Kyle	What the heck was that?
Amy	Shh!
Narrator	Amy's phone bleeps yet again.
Lily	It might be the police.
Amy	No it's not … it's from him.
Narrator	The glow from Amy's phone lights up her terrified face.
Lily	W-w-what does it say?
Amy	It says, "I'm coming to get …"

Babysitter Nightmare

Danny   Coming to get what?

Amy   That's it. That's all it says:
"I'm coming to get …"

Narrator   The wind howls round the house.
The friends hear shouts
and the slamming of car doors.
They hug each other
and wait for it all to end …
one way or another …

Connor   Come here, Bonzo.
I'll protect you.
The poor dog is shaking!

Kyle   He's not much of a guard dog, is he?

Connor   He's scared.

Scene 4   The end?

Amy   So am I!

Lily   Why's this happening to us?
What have we done to hurt anyone?
We don't deserve this.

Danny   I hope it *is* Charlene Smith.
I don't want to be attacked
by an axe murderer.

Amy   Who said he's an *axe murderer*?

Danny   I didn't mean it like that.
I meant … well, you know …

Kyle   It's gone very quiet.

Connor   Bonzo's stopped shaking.
Do you think he knows something?
Do you think it's safe now?

Danny   I'm going to look out of the window …
Hey, there's a car driving away.

Lily   Is it a police car?

Danny   Can't tell. It's too dark.

Narrator	Amy's phone rings. In her surprise, Amy drops it on the carpet.

Amy It's him again.
He's phoning this time.
I don't want to speak to him.

Lily I'll speak to him … Hello!
Yes? Oh, thank goodness. Thanks a lot.
Yeah, I'll tell them. Thanks … bye.

Narrator	Lily looks at her friends' faces and bursts out laughing.

Kyle What?

Danny Come on, tell us.
Was it him?

Scene 4 The end?

Lily It was the police.
They said they caught him outside.
He was writing a text.
They're taking him to the police station right now.

Amy I'm coming to get … you!
That's what he was writing.
They got him before he wrote
the last word, but he still sent it.

Lily Hey! That means we're saved.
Everything's going to be okay!
I need a hot chocolate.

Amy Me too! Let's get out of here
before we wake the twins.

Narrator The friends go downstairs.

Danny I wonder who's winning.

Lily Who's winning what?

Danny The football, of course.

Lily Ugh!

Connor Look! There's another news flash. "Escaped axe man 'The Teaser' has been captured." See, it's true. They've got him.

Amy He really *was* an axe murderer! Thank goodness they've got him. How did he get my number? How did he know I was babysitting tonight?

Lily It's all right now, Amy. It's over. There'll be a really simple answer.

Scene 4   The end?

The boys   Yeah! Great goal!
We won!

Amy   You can all help me tidy up
this place and go.
I don't want the Petersons
to know what's been going on.
They'll never ask me back.
They pay really well.

Narrator   The friends tidy up, and then Amy
shoos them to the front door.

Amy   See you guys. Thanks for being here.
I don't know what I'd have done
without you.

Lily   Are you going to be all right?
We can stay if you like.

Amy No. I'm okay now, and the police have got him all locked up. Bye guys, see you tomorrow.

Kyle Bye, Amy.

Danny See ya.

Connor Bye, Bonzo. I love you!

Narrator Amy changes the TV channel, and waits for the Petersons to come home. Bonzo sits on the sofa with her. He looks at her with loving eyes.

Amy You're a useless guard dog, Bonzo! You didn't bark once tonight.

Scene 4   The end?

Narrator Bonzo sits up, alert.
He growls.

Amy What's up, Bonzo?

Narrator Bonzo barks and Amy's phone beeps
a message alert.

Amy It's all right, boy.
It's probably Lily.
Oh no! It can't be –
it's him again!
What does the message say?

Narrator Amy opens the message
and whispers the words of the text.

Amy *"I'm still watching you!"*

Drama ideas

After Scene 1

- In your group, think together about what will happen next. Who is The Teaser? How will Amy and the others react to the text?
- Act out your ideas.

After Scene 2

- In your group, each choose a character from the play. Imagine the character's thoughts at the end of the scene.
- Take on the role of your character, and tell the rest of the group what you are thinking.

Drama ideas

After Scene 3

- Hotseating: Choose one person to be Danny.
- Everyone else can ask Danny questions, e.g. is he scared of The Teaser? What does he think is the best way to deal with the situation?

After Scene 4

- With a partner, imagine a phone call between Amy and one of the other characters, after the end of the play.
- Is The Teaser still out there? What should Amy do now? Act out your discussion.

SuperScripts

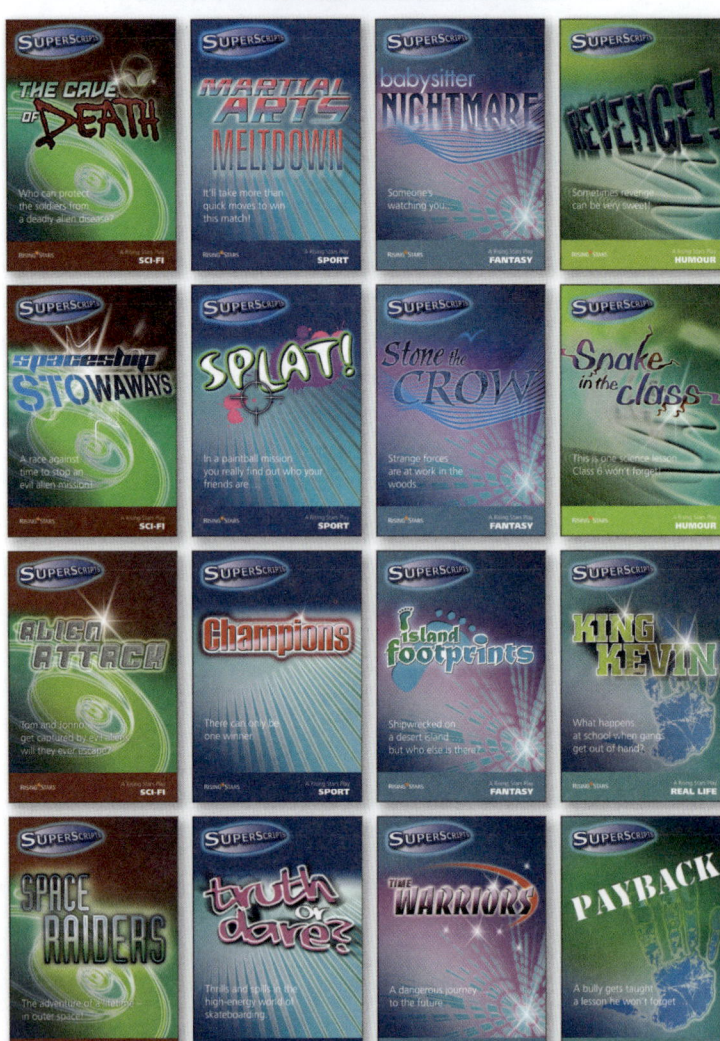

The Cave of Death — Who can protect the soldiers from a deadly alien disease? — SCI-FI	**Martial Arts Meltdown** — It'll take more than quick moves to win this match! — SPORT	**Babysitter Nightmare** — Someone's watching you... — FANTASY	**Revenge!** — Sometimes revenge can be very sweet! — HUMOUR
Spaceship Stowaways — A race against time to stop an evil alien mission. — SCI-FI	**Splat!** — In a paintball mission you really find out who your friends are... — SPORT	**Stone the Crow** — Strange forces are at work in the woods. — FANTASY	**Snake in the Class** — This is one science lesson Class 6 won't forget! — HUMOUR
Alien Attack — Tom and Johnno get captured by aliens, will they ever escape? — SCI-FI	**Champions** — There can only be one winner. — SPORT	**Island Footprints** — Shipwrecked on a desert island but who else is there? — FANTASY	**King Kevin** — What happens at school when games get out of hand? — REAL LIFE
Space Raiders — The adventure of a lifetime in outer space. — SCI-FI	**Truth or Dare?** — Thrills and spills in the high-energy world of skateboarding. — SPORT	**Time Warriors** — A dangerous journey to the future. — FANTASY	**Payback** — A bully gets taught a lesson he won't forget. — REAL LIFE

RISING ★ STARS

PHONE
0871 47 23 010

www.risingstars-uk.com